When women lead

Angela Pride

Contact the author at:

whenwomenlead@coachwithpride.com

Dedication

This book is dedicated to team Pride!

The five people that I can always count on to believe in me and encourage my dreams even when I know sometimes you all didn't understand.

Thank You

Contents

Prologue

Tribute to "Ma"

ഇരുന്ന

My grandmother, Maggie Louise (Ulmer) Smith, born to Sam and Mary Ulmer in Salem Al, and was the best grandmother anyone could ever hope for. She stood only about 5ft and was a very humble and sweet lady. There are not many days that go by that I don't think about her. The influence that she has over my life even today as I place my glasses underneath my pillow, I remembered that's what she did each night.

My grandmother was a true leader. She was one of the best types of leaders, one that didn't need the spotlight. She was the type of leader that was always doing, the type that you are not afraid to follow. I don't believe she even knew that she was a leader.

I remember her being very patient with me. I was a very talkative child (well, at least around my family) and I'm still very opinionated. She would applaud me for things like this. She always found a way to put a good positive spin on my actions. "Oh you're going to be a lawyer one day," she would say, "because you talk so much." When I would tell her I wanted to be a doctor, she would tell me that I could be anything I wanted to be; and I believed her.

I always felt like I had her attention, I always felt loved, and that I was special. She gave me the confidence that I could go out and do anything and most importantly she believed in me and I knew it. Great leaders create other great leaders. She spoke into me almost daily. She told me stories of her life, the good and the bad.

When I was growing up with my grandmother, she was definitely a saved, sanctified, holy Christian yet she never pretended to be perfect. She told me all about her past lifestyle and the things that she used to do; even the things she wasn't necessarily proud of. I respected her for this, her honesty and her transparency. Although I was a very young child at the time; I appreciate her transparency and humility till this day.

I rarely recall her ever complaining. From where I stood as a kid, she pretty much ran the household while in a submitted role, took care of her husband and her grandkids. She did this every day and all day. She didn't want for much. I don't recall her ever making a specific request for anything really. My grandfather shopped for the food that she would cook, and for her clothes. I think she may have picked up her own wigs, but that's about it.

She only had a third grade education, but to me she knew everything. I guess she could have been down on herself because of this but she wasn't. Instead she used it to motivate her grandchildren. I know she instilled in me the importance of school and getting a good education. She always encouraged me to go further and to do more than she ever could.

Not only that, she basically prepared me to do more. She told me how smart I was almost on a daily basis. She couldn't really help us with our homework; actually when I think about it her penmanship was horrible, but she definitely pushed me to do well. So from that I strived to get good grades all the time. I ended up being an A/B student because I wanted to make her proud.

She never learned to drive, but she wasn't afraid to walk anywhere she needed to go. Especially if it meant coming to get me if I was not home before the street lights came on. I remember that just as if it were yesterday. I would be over to my friend's house and had no respect or awareness of time. I would then look up and my grandmother will be headed towards me with a stick in her hand, as if she would ever use it on me. Now that I think about it, the stick was probably more for stray dogs in the neighborhood, rather than the "whoopings" that I never received. This was her way of refusing to allow me to go astray. I didn't understand it at the time, but now with my own kids, I understand all too well. She always shared with me that there was nothing out there in those streets especially not for a pretty girl such as myself.

She really did care and she knew just how to show it. I remember her teaching me how to cook, cornbread in particular; she never yelled or got frustrated. She was always willing to teach me. A true leader, she wanted me to learn as much as I could. Everything she made, she made with love and therefore it was awesome. I never saw her use measuring cups, she just seemed to know. I remember her making cornbread every night because that's what my grandfather wanted. He had to have his cornbread. She made most things from scratch. Late nights, she would make fried green tomatoes (homegrown), the best I've ever had. On some late nights we would have cornbread and syrup.

I loved cheese as a child but my bowels had issues with cheese. My grandmother would never tell me no. She would warn me; but somehow I still ended up eating cheese until my heart was content. I remember all the times when I would struggle to use the bathroom; she would just find ways to comfort me. "Ma" truly knew how to make everything better.

It didn't just stop there though; my grandmother also taught me how to be a lady, how to clean, and how to take care of my body. She also instilled in me how important my body was and how precious it was. She told me how beautiful I was and how important I was. She was so patient with me. This is probably why I expect everyone else to be patient with me as well.

So, with these great attributes, how could I not go far? How could I not be great? How could I not be a leader?

When we moved away to Atlanta, I was 12 years old. I remember crying like a baby because I had to leave my grandmother and she cried too. I can never imagine how that must have hurt her. She was, however, happy for us. She knew that we would have better opportunities in Atlanta, and that is all she ever wanted - the best for her grandchildren. "Ma" never stopped praying for us nor sharing her love.

She had a stroke around 1997 and my mother cared for her until she went on to be with the Lord. I miss you "Ma" but I thank you for pushing me into greatness. I think about you often, wishing you could just speak to your great grandkids. I know you are smiling down on us but, more importantly, continuing to intercede for us all. I find great pleasure in knowing that we will reunite one day. Thank you for teaching me to lead as a girl child. Thank you for teaching me to be a proud leader. I love you, Rest in Heaven.

Introduction

Leadership

෨෨

It's not always as easy as it seems. This book was inspired by my life experiences. I am inspired by the different trials and tribulations, along with accomplishments, that I as a female leader have faced. I've also gone back and looked at other women and their stories and found a lot of similarities so I decided to share.

This book should encourage you as a woman, it should lift you as a woman, and it should push you to keep moving forward as a woman leader.

If you are a male, this book can also be helpful. Many female leaders possess qualities to be admired and emulated. It may also teach you as a male how to relate more to your female counterparts.

Leadership for me is always been about the journey, about the process, and about the experiences. With that being said, leadership has many definitions; it will just depend on who you ask.

If I had to add my own personal definition I would definitely say being a leader is about being the standard; it's about being a good example; a model, doing things others won't have a problem following. I also feel like being leader has requirements.

- ➢ There must be a vision.
- ➢ You must be action oriented.
- ➢ You cannot be a know it all.
- ➢ Leaders actually know what they know, but they also know what they don't know; so they can surround themselves with people who are great compliments to their weakness.

I do believe in natural leaders. Natural leaders are just born with certain characteristics that allow them to lead easier than most. However, in general, most leaders are definitely made based on the things that I mention above; their journey, their life experiences, and so on.

I personally believe that women make some of the best leaders. But this book is not about comparing male vs. female leadership. It is more about discussing and highlighting some of the great qualities that women bring to the leadership table. From my experience, women do bring many different qualities and we tend to execute these qualities differently. Therefore, when women lead, things happen. People around tend to be more curious, cautious, and critical.

Why is this, you may ask? It has nothing to do with the woman leader, of course, but everything to do with the insecurities of everyone else around. I will discuss the fact that women leaders can be emotional a little bit later, but for now just know that when women lead, it places everyone on their toes. Is this a good or bad thing? That is debatable and by the end of the book I hope that you have your answer or at least more perspective.

As a woman leader, I didn't set out to be this different. I started out a little girl who didn't have a clue as to what leadership was about; however, even then I possessed qualities that showed that I was a naturally born to lead so let's begin there.

Chapter 1

The Journey Begins

ഇൽ

I grew up in the small town of Bessemer, Alabama, primarily being raised by my grandparents. Those were some of the best experiences of my life. During those times it took a village to raise a child. My grandparents raised not only me and my brother, but many of my cousins and other family members that dropped by or stayed longer than the weekend; then there were just those that were there all the time.

What I do remember about these times is that I was the baby but it seemed I was always in charge. For the most part, I got whatever I wanted. I was spoiled rotten; but these are all good things right? Well I guess depending on who you ask!

I recall going to the grocery store with my grandfather, who was on a fixed income. He only went to the store on the first of the month, but on that once a month trip to the store he had at least three, sometimes four buggies; ensuring that he retrieved all of the staples that my grandma would need to do the cooking for the household.

My job during the trip was very important; to basically get whatever I wanted and to ensure no one else put anything in the buggies without permission. From this I had my own box of cereal, my own snacks, my favorite cheese and whatever else my heart desired. Those were definitely the good "ol'days". When I look back I know that I was in training. I was in training to become a leader at the young age of at least five or six. I had no clue of even what leadership was then.

Once I went to live with my parents in Atlanta, Georgia. My mother, a nurse, was just as prepared to take over right before my preteen years and she continued grooming me for leadership. As a child, I was never taught that men were better or better leaders or that they could do more. I never saw men as an obstacle. I don't even remember there being in a discussion about male leaders versus female leaders. The goal was always to be out front.

My mother was educated so she knew exactly the path to put me on so that not only could I do well but do better than she had done and achieve my dreams. The journey with my parents definitely took someone of a different turn from what I was used to with my grandparents but what doesn't kill you makes you stronger right?

So Georgia offered better schools and a better opportunity for me and my brother; and I was just leaping at the chance to do great. I always knew that, whatever I was going to do, I was not going to be able to do it from Bessemer, Alabama. So I counted being relocated to Atlanta as a blessing.

My leadership qualities immediately kicked into place. I was leaving an "all black" environment and entering into a predominantly white environment - which for most would have been a definite culture shock. However, my ability to adapt helped. My mother's encouragement also definitely helped me. She also told me that I could do anything that many of the other kids were doing because I too was very smart. I quickly learned that I had communication skills and the ability to basically make others comfortable around me, which immediately allowed me to make friends.

My leadership ability took me out of the typical stereotypes that are often placed on young African American students. So by high school I was on student council and in many social clubs throughout the school, including Future Business Leaders of America.

I was groomed to be a confident, outspoken, educated leader and I really didn't even know it at the time. It's hard to explain, I knew but I didn't at the same time! I didn't know that those were leadership qualities. I didn't know that those were things that other people struggled to accomplish or achieve.

These were things that came naturally to me. These were things that were expected of me. These were things that I took for granted for far too long.

After I began working at the age of 15, it was clear to me that others could also see the leadership characteristics that I possess. I was promoted to lead cashier after only about 8 months of employment at my first job. I was always very focused on doing better; on being above average, and now I know that I was being a leader.

Every job after that was pretty much the same. I always went above and beyond the normal call. I always wanted more. This is a drive that I've always been obsessed with. From my research and study of others, I've also found this similar drive in most women leaders. Most women leaders have a drive that is oftentimes not understandable. I feel like that drive comes from us wanting to prove something - not to the world but to ourselves. So my advice is that we should pay attention when women lead, because class is in session.

Chapter 2
Drive Is A Necessity

ഇന്ദ

When I think about the drive of women leaders, I say that for the most part it is indescribable, but I will do my best.

From childhood, I feel that I woke up with an itch, an itch that I had to scratch. It's almost like I knew that I would be in front of a multitude one day. I can't describe it, how could I know that I was going to do more?

At this point in my life I still remember it so vividly. It was like I woke up one day and I knew that, whatever I was going to do, I wasn't going to be able to do it in or from my hometown. I was going to have to be relocated elsewhere.

Now, for a 7 year old, this goes just a tad bit further than imagination, further than even dreaming. I just knew! So, as I continued to push, so did God. He continued to put me in the right places at the right time. He continued to fuel my drive and make me want to always do more. God continued to keep me focused on growing and getting better. Until this day He keeps me pushing forward.

Enough about me take Oprah Winfrey[4] for example. I'm not sure if you know her story but there had to be some major drive that kept her afloat mentally and physically to accomplish the things that she has thus far as an African American female in the United States of America.

Not only did Oprah grow up in poverty; but at a very young age she was raped, became pregnant, and then lost the baby[4]. She overcame all of this because of her drive and now she's one of the most powerful people in America. Notice I didn't say women, I said people because your drive can and will supersede sex.

Let's look at Dr. Maya Angelou, who also goes down as one of the great women leaders of our time. She too was sexually assaulted as a child, went through periods in her young childhood of not even speaking, and in her early adulthood she even said she was into prostitution[3]. Now she is recognized today as a great author, poet, professor, actress, leader, and so much more. All these accolades came about because she was able to get past the barriers that she faced at an early age and drive through to better times and better situations.

As a leader, I feel that drive is essential, because there will always be barriers or obstacles that you must overcome. However, if you don't have the drive you may get stuck in a rut or in feelings that will allow your current situation to overtake you.

This is why I think that there is a difference in female leaders compared to male leaders. I feel that men are constantly being encouraged to lead, to be out front, and to keep moving; whereas women are often looked at based on our circumstances or our current situation before we're even considered for leadership.

When women lead we are driven to do more. We are driven to overcome, to not allow obstacles and hurdles to stop them from moving to the top. It's almost like the stories that we hear about mothers lifting cars off of their babies. I can only describe it like the switch that only you can turn on or off. Don't suppress your drive and please don't allow anyone else to.

I can remember having my daughter at a young age and not being married. Yes, sure I was afraid; however, she became my drive. I knew that I had to keep going, if not for me for her. I knew that one day I would be able to insist that she not give up because I didn't give up.

Also, women leaders need to be careful to not allow our drive to be misplaced. Distractions are everywhere. They are in place to draw us off track; then we must stay focused and remain on the course.

So if you are a woman who is leading currently or perhaps you know you should be, I believe you know what I mean. I would love to hear your story please feel free to share your story. My contact info is at the end of this book. Take action and remain driven.

Chapter 3

Emotional Pros

ಐ)ೕ

When women lead there are many emotions involved. I'm still trying to figure out how this turned into being a negative attribute.

Emotions are part of life; they are good things. Emotions allow us to relate to one another in a better way. Emotions allow us to see things from different perspectives. Emotions however, need to be kept under control.

Somehow, emotions are often brought up when pertaining to women leaders from a negative perspective. When women lead they tend to bring life to the situation like no one else can. When women lead they tend to be very detail oriented. When women lead they birth things.

Our emotions tend to allow us to be able to communicate more effectively i.e. listening as well as speaking. Our emotions allow us to relate to differences in a better way. It also allows for much more diversity and inclusion.

More and more research is being done to investigate the difference between productivity and revenue when women are leaders versus men. In some of my research for this work, I came across an interesting article that attempts to address the effects of Growth domestic product (GDP) of female lead countries compared to male led countries[1].

To investigate the question, their research team spent three years "building a unique data set from scratch" to capture observations of male and female national leaders in 139 countries over fifty-five years, while also measuring gross domestic product (GDP) performance alongside ethnic fractionalization (EF) levels.

"Diversity and inclusion are not just normative concepts we should get behind because they'll make us feel better," Pearce says. "Our process was about trying to go beyond descriptive statistics to actually compare performance outcomes."

In this article they look at countries with high levels of ethnic diversity often suffer from slow economic growth - unless there is a woman in charge[1].

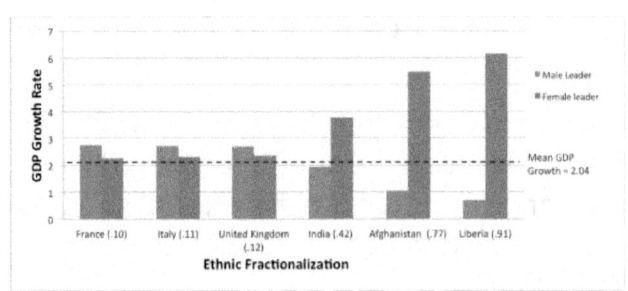

Figure: Point Estimates of Ethnic Fractionalization and GDP Growth Rate for Six Sample Countries[1].
Source: Kellogg Insight and Management - Leaders do matter but when does their gender matter too?

Not only did it seem to be the case that leaders do, in fact, matter, but so too does their gender—at least in countries like Liberia[1].

"In countries with a lot of internal conflict, oftentimes people are looking for signals that the person in charge is going to be collaborative and not dictatorial or self-interested," Pearce says. "Women's gender role is symbolic of collaboration, and they're going to empower marginalized voices." "It's a compelling correlation, but further work needs to be done to figure out what drives the phenomenon."[1]

This is merely an example. I don't mean to get ahead of myself; however, this book is in affirmation for female leadership and our many emotions. My favorite content in this article[1] is thoughts about women being willing to bring others together especially during difficult times; also their roles being more collaborative. This goes to support my view point that the emotions of female leaders should definitely be seen from more of a positive perspective as oppose to always being viewed from the negative perspective.

Some may say that I'm a little biased; however, I can only speak from experience and as long as emotions are maintained and used wisely, they can definitely be a good thing. When I look at the qualities of most great leaders, the ability to show emotion actually enhances many of these qualities. Therefore, I ask why are emotional leaders considered to be a bad thing? This is often also where passion comes from.

In further research and studying of great leaders I learned about Gail Kelly, a South African-born Australian businesswoman. Her story blew me away. Kelly started work at the Nedcor Bank in 1980 as a teller but was fast-tracked into an accelerated training program. She started an MBA in 1986 while pregnant with her oldest daughter and graduated with distinction in 1987.[5] In 1990, she became head of human resources at Nedcor after having given birth to triplets five months earlier. From early 1992 to 1997 she held various other general manager positions at Nedcor, including cards and personal banking.[6]

Talk about being stitched through and through with emotions at this time of her life, she still had the drive and determination to succeed. This is a type of leadership that I applaud and that many women possess.

So be encouraged the next time someone tells you that you're too emotional to lead. Keep moving, stay focus and tell them you'll see them on your way up. Emotions are not a negative part of leadership; emotions actually enhance leadership and don't allow anyone to tell you anything different, keep leading.

Chapter 4
A Few Cs You Should Be Aware Of

శోఆ

When women lead, everyone is more **cautious** as to what's going to happen under our leadership. Caution is not always bad; however, when it means becoming too cautious and everything is being questioned, it will then become negative.

In most cases, being cautious can be seen as being untrustworthy. We all know that a great leader must have trust or they don't stand a chance. This is where being cautious can become dangerous. In these types of situations, a woman leader can spend most of her time on the defensive instead of on the offensive, which is where things happen.

Just because others are cautious of our leadership, does it mean that we have to be moved by this? We have to continue to carry ourselves as the powerful leaders that we are. We can't allow the doubts of others to affect our leadership. There will always be naysayers but we must carry on; we must continue to lead and we must continue to be effective.

Being cautious also brings into play whether a leader is competent or not. However, for all the female leaders reading this, remember this "C": it's called **confidence**.

We must exude the type of confidence so that we gain trust, remove caution, and solidify competence! Confidence is often an issue for many women. Is it something that needs to come across naturally? It needs to reside within us. We need to believe in ourselves; encouraging ourselves, knowing that we are the best person for the job. Confidence is knowing we're capable of reaching and excelling past the goals that have been set in front of us.

Remember, if we don't believe it, how are we going to convince anyone else to believe it? I'm not really sure why women tend to struggle in this area but it's definitely something that we need to overcome.

Oftentimes, confidence is what gets people noticed and we have to know this as women in leadership. The thing that I love about women is that we do it all, whether we have the title or not. So why don't we walk around with that authority? We need to learn to use our multitasking ability to our advantage. It is part of our makeup. Learn to embrace this confidence daily.

The next C that we will discuss is **curiosity**. This is where our gossipers and those that are unsure of our abilities come into play. They speak often about what type of woman we are. How will she lead us, who has she led in the past, and the questions just continue. Where is she from? Is she qualified? How did she get the job anyway? These people often know someone else who they feel was more qualified for the job so they continue to undermine the female leader to make themselves feel better. In most cases they don't even want the job; they just have issues with a female having the job hence the curiosity.

Don't mistake what I'm saying - this person can be male or female. The curious person will always have additional questions. They're always asking something whether relevant or not. Most of the time with the intention to frustrate the woman leader; keeping her on her toes or perhaps off. The attempt is to take her off of her game or to make her seem that she's not capable of handling her load. Curious people tend to be harmless once you put them in their place; that is usually all it takes.

Those that are curious about us, those that present these questions, don't have our best interest at heart. We have to move past this. The curiosity may continue but as long as you are competent and clear in your job and your expectations there are no questions that need to be answered. Curiosity and caution can rattle a lot of women or anyone for that matter, just remember the confidence that has gotten you this far.

I couldn't end this chapter without these two positive Cs: **clarity** and **communication**! Clarity is key. Leaders must be clear in everything that we communicate. Being specific lets everyone knows what the expectations are and what they can expect from us. Be clear and keep it moving. No one is perfect and don't try to be.

Communication is another key in good leadership. Most effective leaders are great communicators; this works well with most women leaders because we are relational. We want to relate to the people that we work with, we want the connection. In most cases it's not just about the title. It's about really enjoying our role as a leader and those that we have the opportunity to lead. Notice I said in most cases not all cases. This is where communication is really important because even if we don't like the people that we're working with; if we are communicating with clarity it's still win-win.

But ladies, we can't take it personally if we don't necessarily get along great with everyone that we work with. Remember we are in leadership and leadership is about creating other leaders, not making friends or developing friendly relationships with everyone that we work with. Therefore my advice as far as communication for women leaders is to keep the main thing the main thing at all times. Don't get too distracted by any one situation. Leadership has nothing to do with making friends. Just trust me on this one. I'm also not saying that you won't develop great relationships in leadership. I'm just saying that please don't allow this to be the main focus.

This is especially important when discipline is a part of the leadership role. Trying to discipline friends is usually a tough thing. All leaders have to correct and or discipline. Keep in mind that we are creating other leaders; which also means examples are critical. Remember these Cs everyone, you will face each of them at some point during the leadership journey.

Chapter 5

Limit The Fear

ೞ◌ೞ

When we lead, women can't afford to be afraid or fearful. We must lead with authority, we must lead with boldness, and we must lead with confidence. There may be doubts that arise for us as leaders, but we push forward towards our goals. As women we cannot allow fear to halt our progress. Our leadership is very crucial to the progression of our great nation.

There are many women that have led in unrelenting efforts and been very successful in their endeavors. I want to encourage you today to be that woman also. Whatever your dreams are, whatever our goals are, whatever our visions are, the challenge is to bring them to life.

However our goals will not come to life if we allow fear to control us. Fear is a tactic that causes us to stumble. Although fear is a natural response to the unknown, it still needs to be controlled so that it doesn't control us. Don't allow it to stop the progression.

As a woman I had to learn to allow my fears to motivate me, to make me stronger. There have been many instances where people have tried to scare me out of my dreams, out of what I knew God had placed inside of me. That is why I can write this today and tell you that if I did it, you can do it too.

Fear often comes in many forms such as; but, or what if, so be prepared. Examples: *"But I don't have the money," "But I'm not educated," "But I don't look right," "What if I lose my job?" "What if I can't get the money?" "What if I fail?"*

Whether we are saying these things to ourselves or hearing it from someone else; be mindful these are just fear tactics trying to control us and/or STOP us. Just because it's thought or even spoken many times, does not mean that it is true. We have the ability to believe and to receive what is the truth about who we are and what we will do. We can't allow others and their fears to dictate who we are, who we will become, or how we will lead.

The first step to overcoming our fears is to acknowledge them. Don't be in denial. Know that the fears do exist but only you can control whether they become real. Call them out for what they are. Then make the move to overcome them. Often when we don't acknowledge our fears they either turn into procrastination and/or excuses, a stalling mechanism.

Now that we know what your fears are, the next step is to make positive statements about them. A statement of how we will take action to overcome them. For example: *"I am afraid that if I start my business it won't be successful, however, I'm going to start my business anyway and it will become successful. I'm going to work hard and I'm not going to give up until it is successful."*

This is called a statement of affirmation. It is also very helpful to write this affirmation statement down and look at it often until we've actually taken the action needed to overcome this particular fear.

The third step is: taking action; pay close attention ladies because this step is very crucial especially for women. What I've found is that we all are very good at multitasking, however; in some instances our multitasking becomes "scattered braininess," which causes chaos, lack of organization, and very low productivity. Our action steps need to be clear and as specific as possible. They also need to have a deadline.

The final step is: gratitude; being thankful that we're able to lead as a woman. Never forgetting whence we came and never allowing where we come from to do anything more than propel us forward.

There is another piece that comes along with the final step which is: Celebration. Celebrate the little things; it's called growth. I don't mean throw a party every time we achieve something. I just mean acknowledge the fact that we as women are accomplishing our leadership goals. I have also observed that when we celebrate, our fears tend to resonate less in your life. Conquering our fears is always best once they are defeated.

When we overcome our fears we must be bold and courageous. Our boldness and courage will allow us to take more risk.

From my experience, I've noticed that many female leaders tend to tread on the too cautious side. What we see in our male counterparts is just the opposite. Men tend to take more risk in leadership, allowing themselves to learn and grow more. We must lean on our confidence and do the same. Fear will make you attach yourself to the strangest things. Complacency is one of those things that we like to become attached to.

I talked in the previous chapter about confidence. Ladies we need to take more risk. We must start putting ourselves out there more. We must allow our boldness, confidence, and courage to grow. Take charge ladies and remember your next level will involve risk. Let go of the fear and Grow.

Chapter 6

We Give Birth

ഇരുജ

When women lead we birth things. We make it happen. My pastor, Bishop Getties Jackson Sr., was the first person I heard put it in these terms. God had a plan when he gave Eve to Adam(2). I believe He knew that we were going to be great leaders; He designed us this way.

Think about it: a woman carries a child for 9 months. Throughout this time her hormones are out of control, eating is totally different, and her body is really not her own, but yet she endures all of this because the end result is oh so worth it.

I know there will be some men reading this that say it's not their fault that God did not give them the ability to bear children, but trust me, God knew what He was doing. I won't even go into the pain that the woman must go through with her bodily changes as well as childbirth. I think you get my point.

Okay so back to leadership concept of women birthing things. We are natural multitaskers and we are relational. We are strong yet emotional. We are nurturers yet authoritative. All qualities of which should be celebrated in leadership. Women also tend to see the gray areas of a vision. We don't look at things as being black and white. This is a good thing, and what makes our ability to birth a vision possible. As women leaders we take the vision and not only help to bring it forth, but bring it forth so that it is a well-oiled machine. We are built to endure pain while birthing things. We are built to be emotional while birthing thing. We are built to protect while birthing things. We are definitely built to help while birthing things.

I would be remiss if I didn't talk about women in leadership from a biblical perspective. When I think about the women in the Bible, the focus tends to be put on how women were seen and not heard. But those aren't the instances that come to mind when I think of women in leadership in the Bible. I think of women being first people at the grave of Jesus. I think of women like Ruth who had amazing faith to wait on God, but to continue to be true to herself while waiting. I see the woman that had the issue of blood being bold and stepping out when she wasn't even supposed to be out in public. These are the types of leaders I want you to focus on when you think of women leaders. I come from a ministry where there are several great women leaders that aren't attempting to do anything but represent the body of Christ.

I think it is important that we not try to be men; but only great women leaders. Women that lead must have at some point on their journey followed. This is that action part that comes into play for any leader. My Bishop says it best "it's not about who you are over, but who you are under".

One advantage that we as women have in this area is that we don't have the testosterone that contributes to the major egos of some male leaders. I think that women leaders possess more balance. We are well rounded, versatile, and we have the ability to connect in several different areas throughout leadership. When certain things need to be done and only a vague description is given, release it to a woman and watch it come alive. Birthing things is all about the actions and abilities of women.

Photo Gallery
of Women Leaders

ഏരു

Maggie L. Smith   Jacqueline Pride

Pastor Anita Jackson

Sharon Black-Smith

Angela pictured here with Black Girls RUN! Founders
Toni Carey and Ashley Hicks

Chapter 7
Never Stop At No

ಬಿ)(ೋ

Get ready because the no(s) will come but we can't stop there. We must be persistent in some cases, we must be demanding but don't take no for an answer. Just ask Cathy Hughes how many no(s) she received while starting her own black talk radio show. She did not give up and now Radio One is worth over a billion dollars.

This isn't the time to be emotional; this is the time to be thick skinned. This is the time to keep moving. This is the time to go get the people in your corner that you know are producers. We must have the mindset that no doesn't mean no, but rather not right now. This mindset, not right now just means there is more preparation needed and more growing to be done.

So what do we do at this point? We keep it moving, doing what it takes to get ourselves better prepared. We push through our growing pains. Then trust me the yes(s) will be ready and waiting. But whatever we do, we can't stop! Don't give up.

There is often a lesson to be learned when you hear no(s). We as women must learn how to communicate better. We need to know what to ask for and when to ask. We must also ask with confidence and be knowledgeable when questioned.

Sometimes I see women that are just excited to be in a position of leadership, they don't expect more. Why is this? We should always have higher expectations. We must see ourselves as deserving raises and bonuses and promotions just as our male counterparts do. Why not us? Because we are women? Should we just be happy with what is given to us? I say absolutely not! We work hard, we multitask and we deliver, but we don't ask.

Let's change this today. It's 2015 and in the U.S we are still fighting for equal wages for women. Why? We have been silent for too long. We have taken just what has been given to us for too long. Today we MUST make up in our minds, make a commitment to ourselves and to our daughters that we are worth more.

I remember some of the nods that I received as I first started my business. People that were close to me looked at me like I was crazy. They didn't believe that I could do it; they didn't believe that I could pull it off. They constantly questioned why I would want to do something like become an entrepreneur.

We don't necessarily need approval when we are a leader. Although approval is good; it doesn't keep us hungry and very seldom does it motivate us. Our true motivation has to come from within. It has to be something that we're willing to go to battle over, sometimes several battles, until the war is won.

Don't misunderstand me no(s) are never easy, but once we overcome one trust me you will overcome them all. This is the part of our journey that makes us better.

Ladies we must prepare ourselves for the transition; learn to pivot, so to speak. Some no(s) will cause us to transition and go in a different direction, hopefully still focused on the same goal, however being prepared for the transition makes it easier.

Being a lover of basketball and having played the sport a bit; let me try to put it in terms of basketball. One of the first things that we were taught in basketball is how to pivot with the ball in our hands. When we're able to pivot it gives us more options.

This is what I mean when I say prepare for the transition. More options are always better when receiving a no. We must always think about our options therefore we're not limited and less complacent. A very simple example of a pivoting option is, as my grandma used to say, "don't put all of your eggs in one basket". Go for the opportunity sure, but don't let it be the start all and end all of opportunities.

As women leaders we must learn to highlight our strengths and minimize our weaknesses. This is what all great leaders have mastered. Being a leader doesn't mean that you have to be the smartest person in the room, you just have to lead.

No(s) will almost always bring about self-doubt. This is when we push through; when we grab the inner strength that keeps us going and moving forward.

I can't close this chapter without a huge shout out to my single moms as well as my stay at home moms. You guys do it all. Single mothers overcome some major no(s) in their life. They often feel like they can't move on from being a single parent, constantly being reminded of being unmarried and the wrongs that they have done in their lives. They are told that there are many things that they can't do.

What most people don't know is during this ridicule is where these women gather their strength. They are true soldiers that rise above the no(s). In most cases becoming much better individuals along with raising beautiful intelligent young people.

So kudos to the single Moms, keep grinding, keep pushing, keep praying, and keep making it happen. You are some of the greatest leaders I've ever seen. You don't get the recognition or the thank you(s) that you deserve.

I just wanted to take this moment to say you are appreciated. Keep moving forward with your families. Keep doing things for your children. Keep leading.

Chapter 8

Don't Be A Hoarder

⚡☙☀☙

When women lead we can't become hoarders. Women are often described as being attached to things, people, and places. In leadership it is not good to get too attached to anything.

Our mindset always has to be creating other leaders. So with this we are going to lose some people as well as gain others. We must become better at adapting to changing situations.

Being a great woman leader means having a very clean and detail-oriented space. I'm not referring to our office space but more the people and the things around us. There will definitely be times when we need to cut people out and let people go. This is what causes us to grow. Think of it as pruning trees. When you prune a tree, the tree grows stronger and with healthier branches and leaves.

The same thing applies to leadership. Never get too attached to any one thing or person. When we become attached to things and or people this stunts our growth. Learn to do whatever is necessary to move on, get over it, or to let it go. The fewer attachments that we have as female leaders, the further we will go.

Hoarding also cuts off our balance. It is important for any leader to maintain balance. Working long hours can also be a form of hoarding. It is something that leaders think is a requirement for being great; however it affects our balance in some of the worst ways.

Unhealthy relationships in the workplace can also be a form of hoarding. We have to keep all of our relationships in the workplace business oriented. This way no one gets hurt or attached, and no one is disappointed. We all know that with attachments also come expectations.

A red flag to business relationship becoming unhealthy is once your expectations change for that person. Expectations can change for the better which oftentimes sets us up for disappointment. Expectations could also change for the worse which sets us up for failure. Keeping healthy relationships are challenging for female leaders because we're emotional and we're just wired different. This is why maintaining a clean space is extremely important in achieving our said goal.

A great example of a hoarder is the person in the office that loves to chat often. This person may be judged according to seniority as oppose to productivity. A hoarder could care less about being an asset. This person is often extremely complacent. We as women have to be careful not to fall into these categories. We must stay ambitious, stay away from the drama, and focus on performance at all times. Because we are relational, some of the above characteristics are easy to submit to; which is why we have to remain aware.

A hoarder will always be okay with no growth. Hoarders will not want to move. They are not interested or concerned with being better. These are all key and important attributes of great leaders; growing, moving, and becoming better. Hoarders don't produce, they mooch. They ride the coattails of others and stay under the radar. They can't stand accountability and just forget about change.

Women leaders we can't allow this to be us. However, if we find ourselves fallen into this status; we must seek help. Find a mentor, someone to push you to be better. Hire a coach to help sharpen those leadership skills and/or achieve higher goals. Go to "your" team, those always in our corner, for some evaluation and honesty. There is always an escape from remaining a hoarder but action is required.

Chapter 9

Choose Excellence Over Perfection

ೞಾೞ

When women lead it doesn't have to be perfect, but excellent. It's never been about perfection, just excellence.

Perfection is not a bad thing; it is actually a good thing, but highly unlikely. However, it can become a bad thing when it halts your progress. I like to tell my clients that excellence is a much more obtainable goal than perfection. After all, no one's perfect right?

Sometimes we as leaders set the bar too high even for ourselves. When we set perfection as ultimate goal, this is too high. I've often heard it said a lot in athletics that perfect practice makes a perfect game. But this has been shown to not always be true. Just because you have a perfect practice doesn't mean you're going to have a perfect game. There will always be opponents that will challenge you, they may just be better than you, or they just may outperform you on one or two plays. This doesn't mean that because we have a good or "perfect practice" our game is going to go the same way.

This same rule applies to our daily lives. This is why I say excellence is a much more obtainable goal. Moreover, I feel that staying the course is also what's going to make you better at being a leader. You may get beat on one or two plays, but as long as you stay in the game and stay focused you will be able to overcome and get back on your "A" game. Trust me, we will never achieve perfection all the time, but we can demand excellence out of ourselves at all times.

Don't allow anyone to make you feel as though you have to be perfect either. We as women face a great deal of criticism and ridicule as leaders. This is okay however, as long as you are secure in yourself, as a leader, and you are meeting your own personal and professional goals, you'll be fine. Aim high always. I wouldn't suggest anything else; however, perfection doesn't allow for mistakes and mistakes are truly one of the largest growth factors in life period.

We don't want to make a ton of mistakes but we do want to have some tangible learning experiences. It is what being hands on is all about. We may be taught by the best but there is nothing like learning from a mistake that propels you into your next level. These are the types of learning one never forgets. Now if everything were perfect, these experiences don't exist. Leadership is one of the best learning experiences. Learning here implies that it's not about being perfect. Remember success does come out of failure but only if you never give up.

Security also doesn't come easily for women, often we feel that we have something to prove. Let me encourage somebody today, if we have this feeling in our gut that we have to prove something, it needs to be to ourselves and no one else. Yes we will make mistake but we will keep moving. Yes we will take risks, even if we fall on our face. The fall is only judged by how we get up. We must have our own excellence standards. We always need to have an accountability partner, someone that we know and trust; someone that will keep us within those standards. So excellence it is ladies. Keep performing at the top of your game and this is what you will demonstrate. We don't have to be perfect to be good. Being good is a practice.

Chapter 10

No Victims Are Allowed

ഔരു

When women lead there are no victims allowed. By victim I'm referring to those that take no responsibility and have no accountability. When women lead there is no room for the victim mentality. This is not the time to play the blame game. This is not the time to dwell on your past. We need to believe that we can do anything that we put our minds to. And we need to walk in that. We all know as leaders it starts in the mind but it definitely goes further than that. It's not just a mind thing; we must be able to walk it out.

When women lead not everyone will be happy or happy for us, go ahead and get used to it now. There will some hard decisions in leadership that are not for everyone to make or be a part of. This is why controlling various relationships is key, especially for women. We have to deal with every decision we make being judged and classified by others. Once we overcome this judgment the sooner we will be able to move. This should no longer continue to be an issue.

People pleasers are awesome, especially when it comes to carrying out vision. In leadership we will not be able to please everyone; we need to say to ourselves "everyone will not be happy or satisfied but this is ok"! We must realize we are not entertainers therefore it will be okay. In many instances women are not given the credit that they deserve as leaders. There are still those that expect women to always submit no matter the circumstances. To me this is laughable and insulting.

This insult brings me to the topic pertaining to control and submission. Women in leadership are often told that they are control freaks. It is always a debatable topic. I feel that women in leadership should be in control and the rest of the world should really just get over it. Often women in leadership are overlapped or often treated like women in the home or in (intimate) relationships. These are two different things.

Most women don't like being under the control of someone that we don't trust or that we don't feel is worthy. I feel that women in general prefer submission (intimate relationships) over being in control but only under the right circumstances. I don't believe that women want to be in control all the time; but I think we want to feel comfortable and safe in the hands of someone else that we can trust to make good decisions for and around us. Is there anything wrong with this?

Submission to me is a form of vulnerability so why would women or anyone for that matter allow themselves to be vulnerable with someone that they don't trust or that don't make the correct decisions for the whole?

These are rhetorical questions; however, women and men allow themselves to submit far too quickly to the wrong leaders all the time. It's done much too often and then we are all too ready and willing to play the victim when everything is said and done.

When most people think of submission they refer to the Bible version of submission which is good. I feel that the Bible is very clear when it speaks about submission but of course, leave it up to (wo)man to twist things and make it about his or her own agenda.

In Ephesians Chapter 5[2] when the Bible refers to submission everyone is submitted not just the woman.[2] Man is submitted to God which means God is guiding his decisions helping him with his choices and ordering his steps and the woman, yes is submitted to man (her husband). I don't think any woman has an issue with submitting when they know that their man is submitted to God but I could be wrong.

I have learned that submission can truly be a beautiful thing and it's not about who you are over but more about who you are under (who's covering you?) This to me simply states that leadership is of the utmost importance. I must include however that if a women is in leadership roles outside the home, those hats should be hung at the door upon entering the home. There should be no overlap between the marketplace and your home. The family is our first ministry and as a Christian leader, I fully support Ephesians Chapter 5[2].

This biblical description of submission from Ephesian does not apply to the marketplace, well at least not in those terms. Unfortunately, women in leadership are often treated as though it should. Submission can and should also work in the marketplace whether a male or female is the leader. In the marketplace women can lead and be just as effective as their male counterparts, meaning they too are just as worthy of others submitting to them.

Moreover, not every leader is worthy of our submission so why should we submit to just anyone? Not everyone is a good leader. Oftentimes males in leadership want women to submit to them when they mishandle their own situations, roles, and lives. So why would any woman want to submit to someone in this predicament. We as women can no longer afford to stand around and be led just by anyone. We must stand for something or fall for anything.

This is why our leaders really should be chosen carefully not just by chance. When bosses are unethical, why do we stay? When managers aren't leaders, why follow? When leaders only functions through chaos, why conform?

I've also learned that leadership has very little to do with control but more about looking at the big picture making the right decisions for not only you but others. I love the saying "when people show you who they are, believe them the first time". Not enough people trust and believe this.

As women leaders, we must stand for leadership. It goes back to accountability, being accountable for our own actions first and then and only then being able to be accountable for the actions of others. As women leaders we must stay aware and not allow others to determine our leadership and or submission. The main key is to stay out of victim mode, stop playing the blame game. Accountability and Responsibility must remain in the forefront always.

Chapter 11

Train Others How To Treat You

ಐಡಲ

When women lead we must train others on how we would like to be treated. We must be intentional when training others how to treat us; however, we have got to be more hands on with our training.

As women, sometimes in relationships we come across so independent because things might be going well for us currently, perhaps it was just the way that we were raised. We are constantly relying on men to be the protectors that we need, and often we live to regret it when they don't live up to our expectations. We must learn to be accountable because in most cases this is the way we were trained to be (independent).

The same is true for men. When men enter into a relationship they should come in as the head or as the leader. Just because a woman is independent doesn't mean that she doesn't want to be protected. It is the man's job to break down those walls that she's built up and show her that he can be her protector, provider, hope, priest, prophet, and King. It is definitely a two way street and hard work. The key is the work.

We all train people the way we want them to treat us. So why do we act surprised when people treat us a certain way, when in all honesty we should take some accountability for allowing them to treat us a certain way?

Hindsight is definitely 20/20 in the experience of life. Think about your current relationship - or about your children if you have them. The way they act or behave around you is the way that you've train them to behave.

Alarms went off for me pretty early in my marriage. I picked up behaviors from my parents that I didn't even realize I had. My mannerisms were affected by the way that my parents behaved. My communication was mimicking the way that they communicated.

I'm sure there's a book out somewhere that covers behaviors and habits, I won't pretend to be that expert. I do know that our brains are like sponges, especially during the early ages of life, so we shouldn't be surprised at the behaviors of those around us. Behaviors are picked up through training. Everything in many ways is all about training.

Have you ever heard the saying that "first impressions are everything"? This is true however they are not the only thing, because after that initial impression you start to train that person on how to treat you. Whether good, bad, or indifferent, we play a very important role in the treatment that we receive from others.

The problem is whether or not we are conscious of the actual control that we have. If a person describes a person that they know or encounter as just rude, mean, or disrespectful. Think about it this way; we or perhaps others have allowed the meanness and disrespect. The relationship would be totally different or perhaps fail to exist if this type of behavior was not allowed. So in the case of a disrespectful mean person, their behavior has been tolerated and this to that person makes it justifiable.

Allow me to summarize my point, let's stop pointing the finger and take a look in the mirror. No one really wants to be accountable anymore or take responsibility for their own behavior which is where a major lack in leadership begins. We are powerful beyond measure especially when we stay in control of ourselves. But if we lose control our fate or destiny will be placed in the wrong hands.

Think about this for a minute. Now think about the bad decisions that you've made. The relationships you've allowed yourself to be in for too long. Think about the bad business decisions that you've made, staying on the job when you know you're not being fulfilled; working for a boss that you know is unethical. Perhaps not going back to school to get your degree or finish up your degree because of what others are not doing.

When people show you who they are really believe them. I'm not really sure why, but this seems to be a breakdown for most people. This is your time to stop making excuses and make the necessary adjustments in and throughout your life. Adjustments are definitely necessary in most situations because if we don't make them now we are just setting ourselves up to become a victim. But we need to take accountability for ourselves instead of just playing the blame game. Remember that training is hands on; it may involve us setting boundaries, saying no, having standards that are not breakable, and having certain things that we just will not accept. All of these things give us the power in our life and control over our life.

When you stay in training mode there are no victims allowed. Victims feel sorry for themselves, they have absolutely no accountability, and they are always throwing a pity party. They tend to stay in victim mode in most instances. So I hope that this message prepares you to get into training mode as opposed to victim mode. Here are some tips to ensure that you stay in control and stay accountable.

1. Self-accountability is always number one
2. Knowing who you are
3. Setting standards that are unbreakable
4. Setting boundaries and not being afraid to use them
5. Never allow yourself to be the victim
6. Self-control.

Chapter 12

Superwoman Is A Fictional Character

ഈ(ൽ

When women lead we don't have to be Superwoman, although sometimes it may feel like it. We are not superhuman, so don't try to be.

We as women we take on everyone else's issues, we take care of everyone else, but we must learn to care for ourselves. We must at some point put ourselves first, and make ourselves a priority.

Because when you operate in superhuman mode 24/7, this eliminates time for you. Please focus on your health, focus on being stress free, and only then can you focus on being the best you. Multitasking is one thing, and one thing that most women often do well. But as I talk about in this book, the importance of **team** cannot be overlooked.

We are not supposed to accomplish everything alone. We should not feel like a one-woman show. We are not any less of a leader because we obtain help. Remember in the previous chapter when I talked about training people on how they should treat us? We can't train others around us that we are the start all and end all of everything. Empower them in such a way that makes them want to do more and then allow them to do it.

Often we as women don't have an outlet, we don't have someone that we can go to and share our problems with in confidence - but we should, we need this. Everyone needs an outlet. Don't keep everything bottled up. Don't feel that you need to carry everything alone.

Figure out when you've reached your maximum capacity. This comes from honesty. This comes from not feeling the need to put on a face to impress others who usually have no relevance or who simply could care less about your well-being anyway.

Drop the faces and focus more on developing your team. Superwoman was a fictional character, not us. Trust me, being the best you is so much better and it adds longevity to your lifespan.

There should not be an overload mode for us as women leaders. It just shouldn't be necessary or tolerated. Aiming for Superwoman is also the biggest invitation to stress. When we try to tackle everything, stress is inevitable. Stress brings about mood swings, headaches, improper rest, and the list goes on.

Sometimes, I admit that it sounds good for everyone around us to applaud the many things that we do. Moreover, we must learn that involving our team and creating other leaders always means that we will be able to do more.

Attempting to be Superwomen isn't being a leader, it's actually the opposite. Everything is about one person, which isn't leading but only walking. Followers are a must for leadership.

So ladies, give up the hero status and become more team focused. Learn to acquire the right help, to delegate, and accentuate our strengths. Save the super heroes for the big screen.

ℰᏧᏇ

I pray that this book has been uplifting to your leadership call. Volume 2 will be available very soon.

Until next time KEEP LEADING!

Acknowledgements

℘℘

I can't thank my husband (Troy Sr.) enough, thanks for being my cheerleader when I needed it. You make me a better me. Brionah thanks for always being ready with suggestions and honest feedback. Troy Jr., Chance, and Trinity thanks for always keeping me on my toes and also for the inspiration.

To my mother, my biggest fan, author Sharon Black-Smith, thank you for always having time for me. Thanks you for your proofreading and editing suggestions. I love you. I pray that I continue to make you proud.

To my Book Coach Elder Leroy Locklear, I really appreciate you believing in me. Thanks for always speaking into me and helping my through the process of becoming an author. I'm forever grateful.

To my Bishop Getties Jackson Sr. and Pastor Anita, thank you for teaching me the true meaning of the word 'leader'. I appreciate you always calling me up higher so that I am now able to walk in my purpose. I love my KAOC family.

To all the family and friends who continue to pray for me and support my vision, thank you all.

There have been so many major women in my life who have helped to shape and influence my leadership journey. The women pictured in the photo gallery are pioneers that have always exuded great leadership and have, in many ways, pushed me to better in so many ways. I am so thankful and grateful for their splendid examples.

Appendix

ဆ)ભ

1. Kellogg School of Management Northwestern University

   Kellogg insight Management and Leadership

   Leaders do matter but when does their gender matter too?

   Based on the research of Susan E. Perkins, Katherine W. Phillips and Nicholas Pearce

2. Holy Bible

   New American Standard Version

3. I know why the caged bird sings

   Maya Angelou

4. Oprah Winfrey Talk Show Legend

   Sara McIntosh Wooten

5. The Australian Financial Review

   How I broke the glass ceiling: Gail Kelly, Westpac

   12 September 2014

6. www.news.com.au

How Westpac CEO Gail Kelly climbed the ranks from bank teller to most powerful woman in Australian business

20 March 2014

Contact the author at:

whenwomenlead@coachwithpride.com

We would love to hear your story!

www.ingramcontent.com/pod-product-compliance
Lightning Source LLC
Chambersburg PA
CBHW070933180526
45168CB00003B/1063